MW00943423

Pra

Boost Your Basketball IQ

"I loved reading this book. It was informative and enjoyable from start to finish. Jason has done a great job of providing players and coaches with ideas and concepts that will help them understand and *think the game* better."

—Rob Paternostro,
7-time British Basketball League Coach of the Year

"*Boost Your Basketball IQ* is without any question a great book for a player, a coach or a parent looking to understand or teach the game of basketball better. In this book Jason takes a deep dive into the basic fundamentals of basketball as well as giving you intel on the more advanced version of basketball. This book is a great guide for any type of player—whether you are skilled, cerebral or athletic, this do-it-all book will make you better at the game of basketball."

— Justin Bowen,
owner of The G.O.A.T. Sports Academy,
former European and NBA Player

"*Boost your Basketball IQ* is a must-read for basketball players and coaches! Jason's knowledge of the game of basketball paired with his passion for coaching makes this book an enjoyable read for all fans of basketball!"

—Dan Horwitz,
former collegiate men's basketball player
and coach, author of *Help Them Up*

"Jason has a special ability for teaching the game of basketball in high-level detail while making it easy to understand and implement. Not only does he know the skills that are needed to succeed in the game of basketball, but he also teaches players why and when they should use their skills in each situation which is extremely important and often a missing component for young players.

"*Boost your Basketball IQ* is a must-read, as Jason is highly experienced and knowledgeable about the game. I work with young players all of the time, and far and away the most common weakness I see is the lack of understanding of the mental side of the game. We glorify shooting, ball handling and athleticism, but we forget how important understanding the game is. This book does an unbelievable job of educating athletes and coaches to give them an edge over the competition."

—Jake Straughan,
skill development and shooting coach,
Shot Mechanics Basketball

"I wish I had this book when I was learning basketball. Jason has done a great job gathering all the important details to help make your son or daughter successful. I encourage you to read this book and discover the secrets to basketball."

—Rob Southall,
Associate Athletic Director, head men's
Basketball coach, Elms College

BOOST YOUR
BASKETBALL
IQ

BOOST YOUR BASKETBALL IQ

How to Think the Game, Be the Smartest Player on the Court, and Win More

JASON CALABRESE

For information about this title, contact:
boostyourbasketballiq.com

Publishing Consultant: AuthorPreneur Publishing Inc.—
authorpreneurbooks.com

Editor: David Sandretto
Cover Designer: Zizi Iryaspraha Subiyarta
Interior Designer: Amit Dey—amitdey2528@gmail.com

ISBN: 9798867176068 (paperback)

This book is dedicated to both of my boys, Colby and Chase, for giving me years of satisfaction, fulfillment and fun, and allowing me the pleasure of coaching you in various sports over every season. You made those years an exciting time in my life.

Also, to my wife Sharon, for putting up with a husband constantly running to games and practices for as many years as I have known you.

And to my parents Carol and Bill for driving me to and from games and practices all those years and helping to instill the love of sports into me.

I love you all.

Table of Contents

Introduction

I became impassioned to write "Boost Your Basketball IQ" after observing a proliferation of local and online basketball trainers specializing in improving basketball players' speed and agility, scoring moves, and shooting ability through either in-person workout sessions or workout videos. While these training opportunities are great for young athletes to increase their physical skills, the common thread that all were missing is teaching young athletes the ins and outs of how to play the game.

As a retired high school coach and now an active youth coach, I have had the pleasure of coaching some very physically talented players throughout the years, and I have started to notice an incredible lack of court awareness from some of the most talented players. I have also had numerous parents comment to me that they love watching my practices because I explain situations, give insights and discuss intricacies of the game that their kids do not get anywhere else and that it makes a huge difference in how they play.

It became apparent to me that there is a huge need for these athletes to learn the mental side of the game along with the physical side of it. As an experienced writer, I thought the best way for me to be effective in reaching the greatest number of basketball players would be to take the knowledge from all my years of experience as both a player and a coach and to memorialize the intricacies that I have learned and shared with my players in a book.

My hope is that the book will not only inspire young players to better understand and *think the game* of basketball, but will also give them the tools to apply the lessons I share with them to real life situations. Also, because there are generally no classes for volunteer or youth coaches to help them be fair and effective teachers of the game, this book provides these coaches some ideas and concepts to help them get them started on a successful coaching career.

As a student of the game since my playing days in high school and college, and a long-time high school coach, I feel I can offer a unique perspective and insight to all who read my book — from players to parents and coaches. I modeled the book after Dick DeVenzio's "Stuff Good Players Should Know," which is more of an A-to-Z encyclopedia of basketball than an actual book. It is my personal basketball bible. Similarly, I designed this book to be used more as a reference tool for particular skills so that the reader can revert back to specific sections as they feel necessary. My intention was to make it a light, easy read to make it enjoyable and not a chore for young players. It has been a goal of mine for some time to share these insights with as large an audience as possible so it can have a meaningful impact among basketball players, coaches and parents, and hopefully be passed on from one generation to the next.

As a coach, I value a player who can *think the game* and be a leader on the court more highly than an athlete who can score, and even win, solely on his physical ability. Basketball IQ is knowing and doing the little things on the court that others overlook. Doing these little things consistently throughout the course of a game and season will help you maximize your talents and increase your success, leading to more wins and championships. Many times, players do not learn the intricacies of playing basketball until they are nearing the end of their playing days. My hope is that this book will teach younger players the value of having a robust basketball IQ early in their careers.

This book is also designed for coaches and parents to learn about some of the ins and outs of basketball that the typical camps and clinics do not have the time to get into, that they can use to teach their players and kids. Likewise, there are specific sections for coaches and parents that players should read to get a better perspective on the overall game of basketball. I am often referred to as a details type of guy, and what I share in this book are some of the finer details I have learned over the years that are not commonly talked about on the basketball court. Some parents and players will spend $150, $250, even as much as $750 or $1,000 to attend camps or clinics for a day or week. At the roughly $15 you paid to purchase this book, I assure you if you take the time to read and digest what is in these pages, you will see an improvement in your game equal to or greater than you would attending some of these camps, at a fraction of the time and cost. I hope you enjoy reading and putting into practice the thoughts and ideas that I share in this book as you work to boost your basketball IQ.

A Note to Players

As to not be confusing and continually switching back and forth I wrote the book as if I was referring to the male tense. This is not to slight female players in any way; it is out of habit from coaching mostly boys over the course of 20 plus years. Obviously when I refer to your man it is whomever you are guarding, whether he or she is a female or a male player. That being said, there is nothing in the book that is gender-specific, so female players, coaches and parents will be able to benefit from all the insight, just the same as their male counterparts.

Below is a position key that I refer to throughout the book:

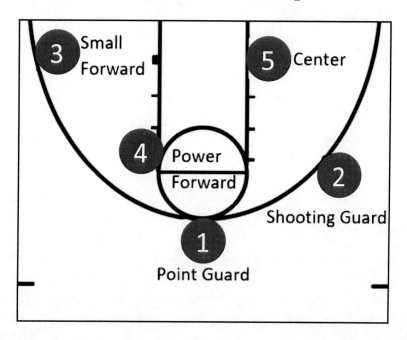

Resources

Be sure to visit www.boostyourbasketballIQ.com/resources
to access larger and more descriptive diagrams than
what you will find in this book.
Use the pass code EXTRABOOST to gain access.

BoostYourBasketballIQ.com

CHAPTER 1

Defense Really Does
Win Games

Defensive Rules to Use

Playing good defense will definitely help your team win games and it will make you a better player and earn you more minutes. When you play consistently good defense, where you make your opponent work for every basket that they get, not only will you limit their scoring, you can also wear them out and frustrate them, causing them to play less cohesively as a team. This will often prevent them from building confidence throughout the game and lead them to taking lower percentage shots as the game progresses, due to their frustration. The great thing about defense is that with some knowledge and effort almost anyone can get good at it. With that in mind, here are seven key rules to help you become a great defensive player. Note that these rules are for playing man-to-man defense, but all of the man principals explained here can be applied when playing a zone as well.

1. Always keep your body between the ball and the basket. I know that it sounds obvious, but you would be surprised how many players neglect to do this on a consistent basis. The easiest way to get burned in a man defense is if you lose sight of your man and he cuts behind you or goes backdoor to an open area. At the same time, you cannot just focus on your man so much that you lose sight of the ball, because if your teammate's man gets by them, you will be unable to help.

   Whenever your man does not have the ball, you should always try to position your body off your man angled in the direction of who has the ball. A good rule to follow is if your man is one pass away be one step away from playing him if he had the ball. If your man is two passes away then you should be able to sag into the middle more to help, but still be two steps away from checking him if he gets the ball. Note this is for regular help man defense. You should not do this if your coach wants you to play man denial defense, in which case you are up on your man and in the passing lanes once anyone gives up their dribble. Make sure when you get in the passing lane to be careful not to overplay the lane so your man can go backdoor on you for an easy layup.

2. When playing man-to-man defense it is much easier to check your man when you get low and wide. There is an old adage in basketball: the lowest person wins, which means whoever gets lower, the offensive player or the defensive player, is going to win that battle. If you're just standing

straight up on defense it's much easier for an offensive player who's getting low to get by you. The second half of this is getting wide, which means stretching your hands out wide at waist level. If you just do a simple test, stand with your hands at your side and you'll see you only cover your shoulder width. However, if you extend your hands out, you'll cover triple the area. Instead of defending the space of just one person, it's the equivalent to the space of three people. Obviously, it's going to make it much more difficult for an offensive player to move laterally twice or three times the distance to get by you.

3. If you get "beat" in the backcourt always sprint to catch up. This is a great tip for playing man-to-man defense full court. A lot of inexperienced players, when they get beat by an offensive player in the backcourt, will slide along with the player. Obviously, this puts them in a bad position because they're not moving straight. They're moving laterally and they're never going to catch up with a guy who's dribbling forward. So, a great rule of thumb is if you get beat in the backcourt, you need to sprint to catch up to him. And then once you get back in front of him, then you should start sliding, getting low and wide and back to playing good defense. If you get "beat" and you try to keep checking him while sliding, you are either going to reach and foul, or you're never going to catch up enough and you will leave your opponent a clear path to the basket.

4. Unless you know that whom you are guarding is left-handed, always use your left hand to try to block a shot. A common mistake many inexperienced players make, simply because most players tend to be right-handed, is

they will attempt to contest or block an opponent's shot with their right hand. Because most of the players on the court are also right-handed, when you go to block a shot with your right hand, you're leaving their whole view of the basket open because they are shooting from the opposite side as your hand. So, to be more effective, try to block a shot with your left hand. In fact, many players are not used to having a hand in their face, obstructing their view, when they shoot because most players always try to block a shot with their right hand. Many times, just by getting your left hand up there in their line of vision, it throws them off enough to make them miss the shot.

5. Whenever you are on defense, you should always keep your hands up. This is especially true if you are in a zone, and when you're off the ball. Just the simple act of having your hands up reduces the angles and windows available in the passing lanes for offensive players to make plays. If you are playing man to man and your man has the ball, you should be low, and your hands should be wide to prevent penetration. However, once your man decides he's going to take a shot, you need to get a hand up, preferably your left hand, or if he gives up his dribble, you need to put your hands up and be all over him. If you are off the ball and the offensive player with the ball gives up his dribble, you need to immediate get your hands up into the passing lanes. If you are playing man defense in the post you need to have your hands up to deter an entry pass. Your goal should be to make your opponent work to catch the ball, not just let them easily get the ball inside the paint.

6. When you are playing defense in the frontcourt (the side of the court that your opponent's basket is on), especially

if it is man-to-man defense, you should only go for a steal when you are 100% sure that you can get it. When you lunge out into the passing lanes and you miss the steal, the offensive player will then have a clear path to the basket and your teammates will have to leave their man to help, which in turn will leave the players they are guarding other opportunities to pass or to score, and make your teammates vulnerable to picking up unnecessary fouls.

7. On the flipside, whenever any offensive player gives up their dribble, when you are playing man, you should immediately get into the passing lanes. Now you can try for a steal, and there is no risk of your man dribbling by you. Just be certain that you don't get too far ahead where you lose sight of your man and he goes backdoor on you.

How To Check a Quicker Guard

If you are playing man-to-man defense and are checking a guard that is quicker than you, there are several steps you can take to limit his scoring. The most obvious step to take, but one that is often missed by inexperienced players, is to play off him when he has the ball. A common tendency is to crowd a quicker guard when he has the ball, but that makes it easier for the guard to attack the basket with his first move off the dribble. When playing off a quicker guard the key is to close quickly on him once he gives up his dribble so you do not give him open looks from the outside. When closing be sure to approach him with your left hand extended unless he is a left-handed shooter in which case approach with your right hand extended. Make sure you stay especially wide to make him have to go much further laterally to get around you.

If the player you are guarding is not the primary ball handler work hard to beat him to his spots when he is running his team's plays. If he is not getting the ball because he is not getting open then you are neutralizing his quickness. Many younger players have either not been taught or do not understand the importance of running sharply and quickly to their spots, so oftentimes you can disrupt them from even receiving the ball, with extra effort. Additionally, you may not have to worry about staying with him as much as when he does have the ball — when he does, it also may be helpful to force him to his weak hand. An easy way to remember how to do this is to point your leg opposite his strong hand up. Specifically, you want to put your left leg up to force someone left and your right leg up to force someone right.

How To Check a Great Shooter (Keep the Ball Out of His Hands!)

The same concept that you use in beating a quicker man to the ball should be employed versus a great shooter. First of all, you are making him work more to get open, possibly wearing him down in the process over the course of the game. Second, you reduce his number of opportunities to shoot. Third, by doing this successfully, you may push him out or to an uncomfortable angle compared to what he is used to shooting from. Fourth, if you are good at doing the first three things on this list you will never let him get into a good shooting rhythm. This may frustrate him and get him to start forcing shots or just stop looking for his shot altogether. In either case, it is a job well done. It is important to remember when he does try to shoot to put your left hand in his face if he is a right-handed shooter and vice versa.

Another way to play a great shooter is to pick him up shortly after he crosses half-court making him start running through his offense farther out from the basket. Constantly try to "push" him out from the 3-point line to keep him from getting the ball where he is comfortable shooting. Some players, with their coach's consent and teammates' knowledge, have great success shutting down a great shooter by overplaying him and sticking to him and by not dropping off of him in typical help defense fashion. This will reduce shot opportunities for a great player but may also sacrifice situations where you could have been in a better position to help a teammate, so be sure your coach approves of this style of defense.

How To Check a Much Taller Guard

When checking a much taller guard you want to pick him up pretty much as he crosses half-court. The reason for this is because you want to push him out farther from the spots in which he is comfortable and familiar with getting the ball. If he is the primary or a dominant ball handler you want to force him to his weak hand. If you are quicker, then you want to crowd him as much as possible without allowing him to drive by you. Once again, when he does shoot, you want to try to block it with your left hand if he is a right-handed shooter and your right hand if he is a left-handed shooter.

How To Check a Much Taller Big Man

If you are checking a post player who has a lot more size than you, there are several ways to cut down on his production and effectiveness. First, you are going to want to physically force him to start posting up higher and at an unfamiliar angle compared to what he is used to. You need to do your work early and you cannot wait until he has the ball in his hands to get him off the spot he wants to get the ball from. A little trick that can help you do this is to firmly plant your foot against his foot closest to you as he tries to get into position to post up. That will send him the message to start to post up where he is instead of trying to back you down further. If he is really leaning or pushing hard on that foot you can strategically pull it away after he gets the ball and he will often stumble or fall enough to turn the ball over or pass it out of the post. After this happens once, he is unlikely to post up as aggressively the rest of game.

Once he does start to post you up you should get your arm around him in the passing lane to deter an entry pass to him. This will take hard work and effort, but when done properly you will see a reduction in the taller post players' effectiveness. The last thing that you want to do in this situation is to sit back and let him catch the ball where he is used to catching from and let him go to work with it. Also, these strategies can and should be used versus a post player of the same or even less height to help reduce his effectiveness.

How To Take a Point Guard Out of His Game

I have found that as both a player and a coach, the best way to take a point guard out of his game is to deny him the ball in the backcourt and force someone else to bring the ball up the court and start the offense. When done correctly, this puts two players in unfamiliar spots and can throw off the opposing team's entire offense. This is because you will likely have the shooting guard starting the offense so he will not be in his usual scoring position, and the point guard will not be making the passes or penetration needed to set up the team's plays. Of course, this should only be done with your coach's consent.

Here is a coaching tip to make this strategy really effective. You can rotate a series of players on the opposing point guard every two or three minutes throughout the game, which will wear him out both physically and mentally. Another coaching note: this tactic demonstrates why it is important for coaches to make sure all of their players and especially their guards are familiar with running the offense from different spots on the court. Limiting a team's good possessions and frustrating their key offensive players often results in poorer shot selection and more turnovers that will add up over the course of a game, allowing less talented players and teams to stay in and ultimately win more games.

Bad Fouls Lose Games

There are many kinds of bad fouls that affect games in multiple ways. When possible, you should avoid fouling someone who is taking a 3-point shot as they will get 3 free throws and if they make the shot they will have an opportunity for a 4-point play. It is never a good idea to foul someone who is taking a forced or bad shot, because they will most likely miss the shot anyway. Why reward them with a chance to make 2 or 3 free throws? It is also not a good idea to foul someone who is far away from their basket (in the backcourt, for example). This is mainly because they are not a threat to score and you are adding to your team's total foul count which will get your opponent into the bonus quicker. If the other team is already in the bonus, it will send the person you fouled to the line for either a one-and-one or a two-shot opportunity.

One of the worst fouls you can commit is an off-the-ball offensive foul that results in either a loss of possession or worse:

the taking of points off the scoreboard if it resulted in a scored basket. Additional factors that make all of the aforementioned bad fouls likely to contribute to losing games are: it gets players into foul trouble which often will limit their time on the court, and can cause players with multiple fouls to play less aggressively, or tentatively, for fear of picking up another foul, fouling out, or being sent to the bench by his coach.

Guards: Remember To Drop to the Middle or Backside in a Zone Defense

A very important action often overlooked by guards playing in a zone defense is to drop to the middle or backside when the ball is on the opposite side of the court. If you do not, you will give your opponent a clear path to an open look in the middle of the lane or on the block. I often see kids, through either ignorance or laziness, stay on the wing or at the top of the key in a 2-1-2 or a 3-2 zone. They get exposed when the offensive player on their side cuts to the now-large open area around the foul line or backside block. Because the basket scored comes from a spot on the court they are not "assigned to," they often do not even realize it is their fault, and it will repeat throughout the game. While coaching particularly younger age groups I can often be heard shouting, "drop" to my guards when the ball is on the other side of the court, to prevent these easy looks from happening.

CHAPTER 2

The Dos and Don'ts of Transition Defense

Preventing the Break Before It Happens

The most important and effective way to prevent a fast break is for the point guard to be in charge of who is getting back on defense, preventing it before it happens. It is not sufficient for the point guard to get back on defense himself; he also needs to understand that when he penetrates or rotates to the wing or corner as part of the offense, he should direct his teammate nearest to the top of the key to get back in his place. He needs to speak clearly, loudly and specifically call out his teammates name to ensure the correct player gets the message to assume the point guard's responsibility of getting back. The conversation should go something like this: "John, you're back," or: "John, I'm crashing, you get back." Point guards: be sure to do this on every possession; being lazy just one time can lead to an easy hoop for the other team and can cost you the game. The other players on the court should also be aware of this and if they notice the point guard has left the top of the key, they should know on their own to get back if they are the closet player to the other team's basket.

How To Properly Get Back on the Break

A key point in playing transition defense that even some of the best players in the world sometimes neglect doing can prevent many easy scoring opportunities for your opponent each game. When you are getting back on defense, run at the player furthest up the court (the biggest threat), not automatically back to the middle of the court. A common tendency is to head to the middle while leaving someone coming in hard from a wing wide open to receive a pass and attack the paint. By simply running at this person you take this option away, and because he was the furthest up the court, you are not giving up an easy basket by not getting immediately getting back to the middle. The goal should be to prevent your opponent's easiest chance to get a basket. Just by doing this, you can slow the offensive team down by a second or two, which will allow time for your teammates to also get back on defense and even things up. At a minimum, if the other team does get a shot off, it will most likely be more difficult than someone cutting to the basket for an easy layup or dunk.

Now, if it is just you and the ballhandler, you should also not just retreat to the paint and allow him to penetrate deep into the lane. If you do, you are giving him an opportunity at an easy eight-foot or closer shot that most players will convert at a high percentage. Instead, attack the ball handler with the goal of either making him change direction or give up his dribble. If he gives up his dribble, you allow your teammates time to get back and help you stop the break. Just getting a ball handler on the break to turn his head from the hoop to the sideline can be enough to prevent him from getting off a high-percentage shot and will give your teammates precious seconds to get back and set up your half-court defense.

When I am coaching in a game during such situations, I will often yell to the player closest to the player leading the break to, "stop the ball," to stop or slow the break. When I teach this concept in practice, I use the phrase, "bump him out," to teach my defenders to attack the ball handler aggressively with the goal of getting him off a direct path to the hoop, or to get him to give up his dribble. **In Chapter 8, under the section on drills, I will describe an effective drill for players to learn this very important skill.**

Always Talk on the Break and Call Out Who Should Get Whom

When you are getting back on the break, it is very important for the first person back (usually the point guard) to direct the defensive effort. This should sound something like this: "I got ball; John, you get the wing." Not only does this organize your team's defenders in the most efficient way possible, it sometimes gives pause to the offensive players because they realize they are not going to be able to just fly up the court, hit their lanes, and score — like they have done so many times before. An important thing to note here is to call your teammate out by name first and then let him know whom to get. This is so that, first and foremost, he knows that you are directing him, and secondly, you do not want to confuse your other teammates on the floor. Another reason to call out instructions using the player's name first is if there is more than one player getting back at that time. You can say something like, "Jeff, you stay left; Anthony, you go right." If you just say, "go left and go right," chances are good that it will, at a minimum, cause hesitation. In a worst-case scenario, you can have two defenders on the left while the player on the right is left unchecked.

One thing that drives me (and most coaches) crazy is to see a player on the other team come down on the break and go right to the hole unchecked while we have a defender back, but he is glued to his man out around the 3-point line. Remember: in a fast break situation it is okay, in fact it is imperative, that you leave your man if there is another player up the court who is a bigger threat to score. Communicating on the court amongst teammates drastically helps prevent this. Once you are able to prevent a fast break basket, your job of communicating is not done yet — now you need to make sure everyone is defended correctly, so you do not give up an easy look. During the haphazard nature of getting back on defense against a fast break, players are often out of position or left checking somebody else's man. A good point guard will say, "Joel you stay with Mike's man," or if you are playing zone, "Ben you stay up — Matt you stay down for now." Then, if the ball goes out of bounds or if there is a stoppage in play, everyone can go back to where they are supposed to be on defense.

Redirect the Ball Handler off a Path to the Basket (Bump Him)

If you find yourself one on one with a ball handler getting back on the break, try to redirect him off his path to the basket. If you can get him to look away from the hoop to the sideline, even if it is just for a split second, it will make your job that much easier, as he will need to refocus on the target before attempting to score. **See Chapter 8 for a great drill you can do with a friend or an entire**

team to teach this very important skill. The same philosophy holds true if you are guarding someone without the ball, but is coming down on the wing. In these situations, you should try to aggressively attack him — even lightly bumping into him, if necessary — to get him off of a direct path to the basket. If you can get him to turn to the sideline for a second, that will most likely mess up his timing and spacing and make it harder for someone to pass to him as he cuts to the hoop. Remember: the more times over the course of a game you can prevent open looks to the hoop for your opponent, the more likely you are to be victorious.

CHAPTER 3

How To Increase Your Team's Rebounds and Limit Your Opponent's

How To Box Out Successfully (Hit and Move)

I have found that as basketball players these days get faster and stronger, and jump higher, the skill of boxing out to get a rebound has become something of a lost art. This is because of the prevalence of players today relying solely on their ability to outjump their opponents for a rebound, versus combining their jumping skills with fundamental boxing-out techniques. In fact, a player who knows how to properly execute and hold a box-out hardly even needs to jump to secure a rebound for himself or one of his teammates.

A very successful rebounding technique that I like to teach players of all ages is called "hit and move." This technique can be broken into four simple steps:

1. **Identify**

2. **Hit (make contact)**

3. **Move**

4. **Secure**

The first step once a shot is taken is to identify which opposing player you will be boxing out. In a man-to-man defense, the vast majority of the time, it will be the player whom you are guarding, or the player closest to you, if you left your man to help out or challenge a shot. If you are playing a zone, it will be the player closest to you who has the best chance of getting the rebound. Secondly, you need to "hit" (make contact with) the player whom you have identified to box out. When doing this, you should spread your legs wider than shoulder width apart, bend your knees, and outstretch your arms to feel your opponent while making and maintaining contact with him using your butt and arms. The third step many players neglect to do, but it is crucial to becoming a successful rebounder. Once you have established firm contact with your opponent, use the power in your legs to move him backward while continuing to maintain contact with him. This creates crucial space for you to get the rebound, especially if you started out in a less-than-ideal position, like directly under the basket. The fourth step is to secure the rebound; because you have held your opponent off and created space in front of you, this should lead to many more rebounding opportunities regardless of your jumping ability or possible height disadvantage.

A positive byproduct of consistently boxing out your opponent correctly is the likelihood of your opponent picking up over-the-back fouls, which may also lead to him becoming less aggressive when trying to rebound for the rest of the game. **In Chapter 8, I will share with you a new twist to a famous rebounding drill that will surely help you master the "hit and move" technique.**

Always Call Out Box or Shot

Calling out box or shot is a fundamental skill that is almost always taught to a player when they are just learning how to play the game, but is often forgotten once they get older. It is also a skill that can be mastered by anyone, but I feel is crucial for point guards as the de facto leaders on the court. Very simply, once a player on the other team takes a shot, yell out **"box"** or **"shot"** to remind and cue your teammates to box out. For one, it keeps you mentally focused on all aspects of the game, and additionally, having ongoing productive communication on the court often leads to success in other parts of the game.

As a coach and an observer of countless basketball games, I am always amazed at how few players bother to communicate with their teammates when a shot is taken these days. Remember: basketball is a team game, and the more a team can communicate and work together, the more successful that team will be.

Don't Forget To Box the Shooter and the Wings

Another fundamental skill I often see neglected is players forgetting to box out the shooter, especially if he is taking an outside shot. Unfortunately, this often comes down to laziness on the court, more than anything else. There are several reasons why that is a bad habit for a player to get into, and should not be tolerated by any coach. Oftentimes, a shooter can tell when and where his shot will be off, so he has the best chance at securing his own offensive rebound, especially if it's a long one. By not boxing the shooter out, you allow him to go after his own shot unimpeded, and you let down your teammates who are working hard to box their man out. Also, you never want an opposing player to feel comfortable on the court; you want him to not only have to work for everything he gets on the floor, but to know in the back of his head that as long as you are checking him, he is going to have to work for everything that he gets, including offensive rebounds. Over the course of a game, this not only wears down his endurance, but it will erode his confidence and aggressiveness as well, and that will give you an advantage over him at the end of the game.

Another common detrimental result of not boxing out the shooter is: by you not maintaining contact/sight with him, if one of his teammates gets the rebound, he is free to cut to the hoop unimpeded, which often can result in an easy basket. Even with the obvious importance of this, it is so often overlooked that coaches and players are often unaware that this mental error led to the other team's easy basket.

A common mistake that I see, particularly in teams playing a zone, is neglecting to box out the wing player opposite the shooter. This is often a crucial mistake as shots from one wing have a higher tendency to ricochet off the basket to the opposite wing when missed. Very often, the guard at the top of a zone opposite a shooter has slid to the elbow and will simply turn and "crash" to the hoop, all but forgetting his opponent left "free" on the wing. It is important to identify any "free" players on the wing and work to get to him before the ball does, so you can make contact with him and move him away from any long rebounds that you can now secure for yourself.

The "Free Rebound"

There are not many players who know how to take advantage of the opportunity to almost always secure a defensive rebound on a free throw. If this is done correctly by yourself and your teammates, it almost always works, which is why I call it the "**free rebound**." Below is a sketch of how it is carried out.

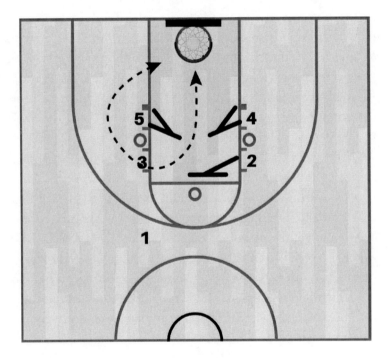

This is effective because of a numbers mismatch that works in your favor. The team on the defensive side of the court has four players to box out three, one of whom is shooting. On the release, the team's two best players at boxing out, generally the 4 and 5 men, need to box and hold off the offensive player on their side of the lane using the "hit and move" technique (explained previously in *How To Box Out Successfully*). The 2 guard needs to slide in front of the shooter to box him out, keeping him from following his own shot. A recent (at the time of writing) rule change does not allow the 2 guard to initiate contact with the shooter, so be sure to spread your arms to feel and be able to slide in front of wherever the shooter is headed. Now for the "free" part: the 3 man has nobody left to box out so he is "free" to go to wherever the rebound is headed. Most players will instinctively just "crash" to the middle of the lane hoping for the ball to come off the front of the rim, but this rarely happens, and they miss out on a great opportunity for a "free" rebound. The key for the 3 man to be successful is to pause a second to read where the rebound is headed, and then to either get in front of or slide around his teammates to that spot. If your teammates are all doing their part, the rebound should be "free" for you to grab.

I still occasionally play in a men's league and even though more often than not I will be the smallest player on the court, I will often use this concept successfully. Just for sport, before a free throw I will tell my taller teammate to get the shooter because I'm going to get the rebound, which will often elicit a head shake, snicker or eyeroll from the shooter — until, of course, I end up with the ball in my hands. My teammates tend to get a big kick out of this when it happens. Of course, for this to be successful, it has to be a team effort, and the other three players involved need to execute their parts.

Visit www.boostyourbasketballIQ.com for a free video that goes over the "Free Rebound" in further detail. Use the pass code EXTRABOOST to gain access.

CHAPTER 4

Pointers for Point Guards

Taking Control

One of the biggest indicators of an effective point guard is his ability to take control of his team not only on the court, but in the locker room, during practice, and off the court. During practice, he should be an extension of the coach on the floor. He can do this by ensuring that his teammates are in their correct positions, that he himself is working to the best of his ability, giving a high level of effort and leading by example — not fooling around or getting sidetracked. Doing all of this will earn him the respect of his teammates and make him effective at being able to communicate what the coach expects of his teammates while he's directing them on the court.

Most coaches rely on their point guard to call out the plays on offense and set their defense. This means that they need to know not only where everyone should be in each instance, but they need to be able to direct those out of place to the right spot during a game. Point guards control the game flow and the pace of a game and they sometimes need to switch it up when necessary to benefit their team. For example, if your team has had multiple possessions in a row without scoring because your teammates are taking quick or bad shots, as a point guard, you could slow the ball down and direct your team to take their time for a good shot. Another example is if your team is having difficulty scoring against the setup defense, instead of walking the ball up and continuing to try to score the same way you haven't been having success with, the point guard can start to push the ball and try and get a look before the defense sets up.

Probably, the most important time for a point guard to take control is at the end of a close game, particularly when his team is ahead. In this case, it's very important that he controls the ball, keeping it in his hands or the other primary ball handlers' and good foul shooters'. This prevents the other team from fouling a poor free throw shooter or getting a steal.

Key Words To Call Out During a Game

With the point guard being an extension of the coach and the leader on the floor, it's very important that he communicates throughout the game. There are several key words that he should call out to alert his teammates at different points in a game. The first one would be either **"box"** or **"shot"** when an opposing team takes a shot. This alerts teammates who may not have seen that a shot was taken because they were checking someone else and their back was turned. They then have the chance to turn around and box out before the other team gets an offensive rebound.

Another one is **"back,"** which should be yelled whenever your team misses a shot and the other team secures the rebound. You do this to make sure your team gets back on D to prevent a fast break. Two additional words to call out while on defense are **"switch"** and **"help."** You should call out **"switch"** if the person that you are checking runs you into a screen and you can no longer check him. This alerts the defender nearest to you to switch off of his man to get your man to prevent an easy open look. You can also tell your teammates to switch (using their first names to avoid confusion) if they don't recognize that they are about to run into a pick. You should also yell out and let them know **"pick right"** or **"pick left"** if there's a pick coming, to give them the direction that the pick is coming from, so they can avoid it. Additionally, you can yell **"help,"** which is to instruct the defender closest to a player who is penetrating to step up and help. Sometimes they just need that reminder to get there.

What's Your Hurry?

A lot of players, once they receive the ball, will instinctively and immediately start dribbling and attacking the basket. Or, if they're in the backcourt against the press, they start to instantly move up the court. Typically, this is done without taking even half a second to simply scan the court, and look. Many times, you can prevent a turnover by not dribbling right into a trap or a waiting defender. You can even find an open teammate just by taking the time to look, which can lead to an easy basket or an easier way to break a press. Additionally, players will often rush getting up the court on offense — particularly the primary ball handler, who is generally the point guard — which leads to bad or rushed shots. Unless you're losing near the end of the game, there's no reason to rush, unless you absolutely need to.

A point guard should know when to take time to set the players on the court where they need to be, ensuring everybody is in the right spot, in order to execute a play. It's okay if it takes an extra second or two to get the play started. There's no reason to just rush for the sake of rushing because that will often lead to bad shot attempts. Your teammates might speed up what they're doing and force or rush shots that they normally wouldn't take, had they been settled down and in their correct spots. It is always good to be confident where and when you want to attack the hoop, and on which play, and it's okay to take your time to know that. However, do not make the mistake of always adhering to this. There are times you need to be aggressive, like in an open court or broken play situation, when it is best to aggressively attack the hoop.

How To Get Open Every Time Versus Man Pressure

It drives me crazy as a coach to watch point guards or primary ball handlers struggle to get open versus a press, especially a man-to-man press. Oftentimes, I will see the guards who are trying to get open run very close to the player taking the ball out of bounds, which really doesn't give his teammates enough space to make a pass. If they can get the point guard a pass and he catches it, he is usually right up against the sidelines, basically creating a trap for himself. It is effectively adding another defender, making it a really poor way for you to execute getting open versus a press.

What the smart ball handler and a good point guard will do is to start at least at the foul line extended. You also should make sure that your defender is behind you. Your first move should be to face your defender and drive him hard toward your basket, then plant and come directly back to the ball. This will create all the open space that you need for the inbounder to safely get the ball into your hands. Another similar tactic you can use is to start at half-court and once the inbounder gets the ball, flash hard toward him with your defender trailing you. Receive the ball, turn, square up, and you are now ready to bring the ball up. Successfully getting the ball into your hands is half the battle in breaking a press; the next section will give you multiple ways to bring the ball up once it is in your hands.

Three Ways To Bring the Ball up Versus a Man Press

1. Once you get open and receive the ball versus man pressure, there are three great ways for you to attack the defense and get the ball over half-court. The first thing you should do once you catch that ball is to turn and face up on the defender. Next, take a quick look of the area, let your teammates clear out, give yourself some space, make either a quick crossover or a sweep, and then attack up the court.

2. The second option you can do is, again, turn and face, wait for everyone to clear out, and then do what's called the spin-and-protect dribble. You dribble up to your strong side with your opposite hand protecting the dribble, and then when you get near the sideline, switch hands, spin, then put your other hand out to protect your dribble and go the other way, creating a kind of zigzag up the court. It's very difficult for your defender to get a steal without reaching in and fouling you, if you properly protect your dribble.

3. The third way is for more advanced players who are going up against a pretty skilled defender. Face up, take two

hard dribbles up, attacking your defender — getting him to go back on his heels. Then, take a dribble back, and as soon as your defender comes back to attack you, cross him over. A good way to remember it is: two up, one back, cross. That is a move that works a tremendous amount of the time. It will get your defender weary of getting beat, and eventually he'll just back off you, and all you really need to do is get open, turn and face, and you won't have an issue with someone pressuring you up and down the court the rest of the game.

CHAPTER 5

How To Increase Your Scoring

The NBA is Fantasy

The NBA is filled with many exceptional and incredible shooters at this moment, like Stephen Curry and Trae Young, but if you're a middle school or high school player, you should not be practicing or even taking shots as soon as you cross over half-court just because you see guys in the NBA doing it. First of all, it is not a high percentage shot, so why take a shot so far away from the basket when even three, five or ten feet closer, you'll have a much better chance of making the shot? It's not like they give you extra points for taking a shot that far away.

If you want to improve your scoring, besides the obvious (taking better shots), you should work on improving your free throw shooting and making your layups. Free throws and layups comprise a large portion of the overall points scored in a typical game and surprisingly few players take them seriously enough. It could affect not only their overall scoring, but the outcome of games. A team that shoots 50% or less from the free throw line in a game is much more likely to lose than a team that's shooting close to 90% from the line.

If you notice that most of your points only come from outside shots or three-point shots, then you should work on other parts of your game like layups or free throw shooting. Conversely, if all you're making are layups and free throws, then you should concentrate on improving your three-point shot.

The Best and Easiest ISO Moves

I frequently see teams playing versus a man-to-man defense and the coach will call an ISO for the point guard or whoever is handling the ball at that time. Invariably, that player will start dribbling all around, doing all kinds of fancy moves and taking up a lot of time without actually making a move toward the hoop. Ultimately, what usually happens, in the course of doing all these fancy moves, he loses control or does something like dribbling it off his own foot, creating a turnover. Or, he eventually makes some move to the basket but he's so off balance or tired out at that point that it's not a high percentage shot. However, smart ballplayers that just want to score will walk the ball up, wait for everyone to be clear, and then make one quick, sudden move. It could be a crossover, an in-and-out, or a hesitation; then they will attack directly at the basket and try to score or draw enough contact for a foul to be called.

The Best Time for an In-And-Out Dribble

The in-and-out dribble has become hugely popular in recent years, thanks to NBA stars like Kyrie Irving and Kemba Walker. One of the best times to use an in-and-out dribble (besides the

ISO discussed in the previous section) is during the open court in transition. When your defender is backpedaling, go right at him and do an in-and-out, and a lot of times that player will actually stumble and fall, leaving you a clear path up the court or to the basket. You can become very efficient at this move by practicing in-and-out dribbles at game speed across the length of the court, and finishing off with a layup after your last rep.

Drawing Contact to Help Your Scoring

A great way to increase your scoring, especially for a poor shooting night, is learning how to draw contact. Being able to draw contact without being charged with an offensive foul is a skill that takes practice to get good at. When trying to draw contact you should always lead with but never dip your shoulder, by leaning into the defender while shooting. If you have a good shot at the basket, there's an opportunity for you to get a 3-point play. In addition to that, there's also an opportunity to get an opposing player into foul trouble.

I would like to add a note for coaches here. A philosophy that I subscribe to as a coach, especially in the second half of games, is to try to get my team into the one-and-one before my opponent's team is in the one-and-one. It's kind of like a game within a game. The reason for this is two-fold. First, if you are leading at the end of the game then you don't need to shoot, and the opposing team has to foul you to try and get the ball back. You will have the opportunity to make them pay by going to the foul line and being able to make one, if not two, baskets in the one-and-one. The second reason is if you are losing in the second half and you're in the one-and-one, you could get fouled or draw contact even in the backcourt and actually score points while the clock is stopped. Also, if you had a hard time scoring all game, you do not even need to beat the defense, because you're scoring from the free throw line.

As a point guard or primary ball handler at the end of the game, if you are leading and in the one-and-one, you should take every opportunity to get and keep the ball in your hands, especially if you are one of the better free throw shooters. It is also important to protect the ball and take no unnecessary risks in these situations. Once it is apparent the other team is going to try and foul, cover up the ball with both hands to protect it so they don't get a steal, and let them foul you. And now you can go to the free throw line and score to put the game out of reach.

Stay on Your Line of Attack

There are two important key points to practice and remember when you are attacking the hoop off the dribble. The first is to move your defender off your line of attack. This can be done as simply as a head fake or a jab step. Other ways include using a sweep, an in-and-out dribble or a cross-over dribble. The second point is once you move your defender off your path to the basket, attack as close to a straight line as possible to the hoop. This will put you in the best position to get off a high percentage shot, and consistently doing so will result in more points and foul shot opportunities for you. When practicing this, be sure to incorporate both parts of the concept: moving your defender and then attacking in a straight line to the hoop.

The Dos and Don'ts of Free Throw Shooting

One of my biggest pet peeves with players who are not good free throw shooters is what they do prior to taking the shot. The first thing you should always do is line up on the nail mark. Most, if not all, basketball courts will have a nail mark at the center of the free throw line, and you should line up your same foot as your shooting arm right on that nail, so you are shooting directly at the hoop. You should not line up in the middle of your stance because if you do, your shot will be off to either the right or the left, because your shooting arm will not be exactly perpendicular to the hoop.

The second thing I often see is that players will take warmup dribbles, and they'll be watching their dribbles and looking at the floor. Then, suddenly, they will pull their head up and try to shoot, without setting a target and focusing on it. This makes it a much more difficult shot. It's actually like shooting at a moving target. Comparatively, if you were catching a ball on the wing and setting up for a jump shot, you wouldn't look at the floor and then try to take a jump shot, and then look at the rim. You would first catch the ball, focused on the rim the whole time, then take the shot. That's exactly how you should shoot a free throw. It's okay to take dribbles before attempting a free throw, just be sure to look at the rim and not the floor when you do.

Most of the better free throw shooters develop a consistent routine they use every time they go to the free throw line. This consistency will allow you to build a rhythm and confidence in your shot so you can focus on putting the ball in the hoop and not on what you are doing before you shoot. A little trick I use to teach the players I coach — and one that I use myself when I play — is to say this in my head when I get to the free throw line: "one, two, deep breath, follow through." The "one, two" are dribbles, which I follow with a "deep breath" that relaxes me before I shoot, and the "follow through" is what I do after I shoot. This relaxes me and puts me into a nice rhythm as I shoot.

Additionally, after you shoot the actual free throw, a lot of players tend to lean backward. If you do that, it will affect your follow-through. Remember to always follow through until the ball goes through the net. If you incorporate these four steps, I guarantee that your free throw shooting percentage will increase, which will increase your overall scoring, and your team will win more games. **See my web extra for a more in-depth video on free throw shooting at www.boostyourbasketballIQ.com. Use the pass code EXTRABOOST to gain access.**

Know What is a Good Shot

I teach my players how to know what a good shot is using a scale from one to ten, with one being the absolute worst shot you could possibly take and ten being a wide-open dunk by Kevin Durant. So, I tell my players, "none of us are Kevin Durant, so I don't expect any of you guys to be taking tens, but I do expect you to take shots that are sevens, eights or nines on almost all occasions." So, what is a seven, eight or nine shot? That's a good shot where you are on balance, there are no hands in your face, your shoulders are square, you're in range, and you have adequate time to shoot without being rushed — whether it is a jump shot or a layup. Now, what's a five or six shot? Those are so-so shots that may work in practice, but not necessarily in games. All it may take to avoid this quality of shot is an extra pass to a teammate. They may have an eight or nine shot at the ready. A three or four shot is, simply put, a bad shot. They are low percentage, and everyone (including you) knows that you shouldn't be taking them. If you want to have a winning team, you cannot be taking many three or four shots during the course of a game. There may come a time when there's time running out at the end of a quarter or a half, and you've got to chunk a shot up that's not so great, but you're just trying to get something up. That's acceptable. Finally, there are one or two shots, which are shots that will lose you games if they are consistently taken. These are terrible shots where you are not on balance, you're not in range, and you have a defender close on you. These types of shots will generally earn you a seat next to your coach; they should only be attempted as a last resort if the shot clock is running out or the game is ending.

The importance of knowing what a good shot is and consistently taking shots that are rated seven or higher can be found by studying analytics of winning NCAA teams. Of all the various stats available these days, the number one correlation with wins in NCAA games is the team that has a higher field goal percentage. This is similarly true for youth and even NBA games. So, it stands to reason that teams that consistently take more higher percentage shots will ultimately have higher field goal percentages than their opponents in most games, which will translate into more wins and a successful season.

CHAPTER 6

Perfect Practice Makes Better Players

The Best Way to Practice (Game Speed)

Too often, I see players practice at around 50% of the speed they will typically be moving at during a game. By practicing in this manner, once they get into a game with everyone moving quicker, it will cause these players to be hesitant and less confident, and lead to ineffectiveness. The opposite is true of the players who push themselves when they practice, at game speed or faster. Oftentimes these are the players for whom things come easier in a game, and these players are usually not flustered by quicker/faster opponents. For example, you should not work on taking layups at half-speed because you will very seldom take them at half-speed in game. This is true even if you make more in practice, because you are going at half-speed. Instead, focus on moving at the speed you will be going if someone is trying to track you down during a game. This will better prepare you for when the opportunity arises during a game. This holds true for everything that you work on in practice, for the same reasons. **See the drill, "layups with a chaser," in Chapter 8 to help you master this skill.**

Go to the Videotape
(Record Your Games and Practices)

This opportunity to help you improve pretty much did not exist for non-professional or collegiate athletes until the advent and widespread use of smartphones about 10 to 15 years ago. Now that the smartphone age is here, almost everyone has access to a video recorder (usually residing inside their pocket), a tool that can help you improve tremendously. Have a sibling, a friend or a parent record your practice workouts to make sure you are using the correct techniques and exhibiting the right amount of effort. Also, see if they can record all or part of your games, then go back and review these videos to see how you are performing on the court and to be able to pinpoint areas of weakness that you need to work on. Some examples of things to look for in games are: did you box out, is your shooting form correct, and are you performing the other skills and techniques that you have learned from this book?

I highly encourage coaches to also take advantage of this technology as it is a great way to pinpoint deficiencies and reinforce the skills you are teaching. I have found even just a half an hour of occasional film review to be as productive for positive results as a full two-hour practice. Heck, in today's world, you can even email a specific player a snippet from the game with a blurb on what you want him to see that he either did right or did wrong.

Look to Take Good Angles to the Square

Whether you are taking a layup, a bank shot or a floater from the wing, look to square your shoulders so you release the ball at a 90-degree angle to the backboard. It is critically important to do this to increase your shooting percentage. On many shot attempts, especially when penetrating into the lane, players find themselves off-balance from avoiding defenders, and neglect squaring their shoulders to the hoop before getting off a shot. By squaring your shoulders (even if the rest of your body is not square) to the white square on the backboard on your release, you will have a much higher chance of making the shot. This is particularly true when taking a layup in traffic, so it is important to practice taking layups from different areas of the court, and not just from the wing — from where you usually take your warmups before a game. One of the hardest layups to make is the straight-on layup just from the right or left of the hoop; if you do not angle your shoulders to the square before your release, the ball is going to come right off the backboard for a miss. **See the drill, "sharp angle finishes," in Chapter 8 to help you master this skill.**

Layups Matter!

One error many players make is to not take seriously enough the skill of making layups in a game. This goes for big men inside as well as guards filling the lane on the break. Believe it or not, oftentimes the most missed shot in youth and even some high school basketball games is the layup. Think about this for a minute: if a team misses 10 layups in a game, that is 20 points that the team is not getting. That can turn an 8-point loss into a

12-point victory. My advice to coaches and players is to be sure to spend enough time mastering the layup and stop leaving those points on the floor.

Some keys to making more layups are: 1. Stay low to the ground on your approach and explode to the hoop when you shoot. 2. Square your shoulders to the white square on the backboard at an angle of 90 degrees on your release. 3. Make your release high and soft. Start by practicing aiming for the top corner of the square, and as you master that, attempt to shoot them higher and higher up to avoid having them get blocked. Players who master the layup will see their scoring averages go up and coaches who emphasize it will see their win percentages increase.

Effort Always Stands Out

One thing any basketball player can do to help their coaches and teammates view them in a positive light is to give great effort every time that they step on the court, for practice or games. A player who is always hustling, diving for loose balls, and sprinting to get back on defense, is a valuable member of any team — even if he is not the best scorer or shooter on the team. Coaches, fans and other players always take notice of a player who gives this type of effort throughout the game. If you want to build a name for yourself while you work hard for your offensive game to develop into a better or elite level, be the guy on your team who gives the most effort. You will stand out in a positive way and that can only be good for you and your team. Then, when you polish the rest of your game, the good habits that you have learned will make you a well-rounded and valuable member of any team going forward.

See Chapter 8 for a list of trainers and resources that I recommend.

CHAPTER 7

Tips for Winners

Be Relentless

One trait many prolific winners possess is relentlessness. Now, it's important to note that this does not just mean being relentless in the actual physical aspect of the game while you're on the court. It is also being relentless in your pursuit of excellence in your craft. Be relentless in your preparation. Be relentless in the way you practice. Be relentless in how you encourage your teammates, and so on and so on. Being relentless in as many areas as possible will help increase and almost ensure that you are a winner in not only the sport of basketball, but in life.

Be Reliable

Another trait most winners have is reliability. You want to be reliable on the court so your teammates can trust that if they throw you the ball, you will catch it. They can trust that if you're open for a shot, you will knock it down, or at least you will take a credible shot and not do something unreliable with the ball. You want to be reliable in practice, always working hard, always showing up on time. You want to be reliable to your coach by being someone he can count on as a leader, and showing leadership by how hard you practice. Your reliability should cause your coach not to have any worries about putting you into a game or in a tough situation. This trait will also translate well for you once you get older and start working a job.

Accepting Responsibility for Turnovers or Bad Shots

A good trait to develop and work on that most winners possess is accepting responsibility for turnovers or bad shots. When you make a turnover or take a bad shot in the game, your teammates can become deflated, they can get frustrated and annoyed. This is especially true if you don't own up to it, or if you deflect the blame to others. A good teammate, a great leader, and a winner will accept responsibility and say, "that was my bad," or, "that's on me," or something of that sort. It will build trust and camaraderie between yourself and your teammates. You'll earn the respect of your teammates and your coach will appreciate it as well. Like the previous two, this is a trait that will serve you well later in many other life experiences.

Ahead Late in the Game

There are three important keys for winning players, and thus winning teams, when you are ahead near the end of the game. The first is that possession is everything. It's very important for you to understand that keeping possession of the ball above all else is the biggest key into you eventually winning the game. If you don't give the ball up, the other team doesn't have an opportunity to score and get back into the game. So, this is not a time to make risky (50/50) passes. We will get into that in the next section. It is not the time to take bad shots. It is definitely a time when you take care of the ball and you're very conservative with it. In fact, even if you're up by one point with a few seconds to go in the game and you have a breakaway layup, it is far better to dribble the ball out than to try and score and give the other team an opportunity to tie it in the waning seconds.

Another important key while ahead late in the game is to know the situation. You should know whether the other team is in the bonus yet or the double bonus. You should know who on your team is a good free throw shooter and you should see to it that the ball gets into his hands. If you are the better free throw shooter, you should do all that you can to keep the ball in your hands while maintaining possession and not doing anything risky that would turn the ball over. Likewise, if your opponent has the ball and they are not in the bonus and they're trying to score, it may make sense in certain instances to foul them before they have a chance to take a three where they could tie a game late. The best they will be able to do is go to the foul line with a one-and-one. Even if they make the first, they will then have to intentionally miss the second, get the rebound, and then score just to tie it up.

Also, if there's a shot clock, be aware of the time remaining and use it all. You want to work the shot clock down to the point where there's little time left, but not to the point where you're rushing or forcing up a terrible shot. If you get an open look, like a wide open three with a good shooter — or if you get an open layup for one of your inside guys — go ahead and take it if there's a shot clock. If there's not a shot clock, it depends on how much you are up by and how much time is left. This leads right to the third key, which is to not take chances. Being ahead late in the game is not the time to experiment and try the new fancy shot in the lane you have been working on. It's the time when you keep the ball in your best ball handler's hands and your best free throw shooter's hands. It's not the time to try a long homerun pass, unless a guy is wide open. It is definitely the time to be conservative with the ball and take care of the ball and secure a victory.

Sure Passes Versus Maybe Passes (50/50 Passes)

Everyone on the basketball court needs to pass from time to time, and everyone should know the importance of possessions and having the ball. So, one of the things I like to teach the players on my teams is the concept of making sure passes versus maybe passes. First of all, what is a maybe pass, or what I like to refer to as a 50/50 pass? I like to call it that because it has a 50% chance of getting to your teammate (or where it needs to go) without being intercepted by the other team and resulting in a turnover. A sure pass is almost guaranteed to get to your teammate (or where it needs to go). So, if you can concentrate on only making sure passes, and if all your teammates do the same, then you are going to drastically cut down on your team's unnecessary turnovers from making poor/maybe passes.

There's no reason to try and force a ball that you know only has a 50% chance of getting to its intended destination. The odds don't make sense, but I constantly see kids try to force an impossible pass. When I ask them why, the usual answer is, "if it got there, it would have been an easy basket," or, "it would have looked pretty." The problem with that approach is that when you do that several times a game, even if you connect on one of them, you are not going to connect on the majority of them. And each turnover results in an additional opportunity for your opponent to score.

Use Your Hands to Make a Target When You Cut to the Ball

A simple habit to incorporate into your game that will save you from many turnovers is to use your hands to make a target whenever you cut to the ball. Too often, I see players cut to the ball with their hands at their sides, and inevitably, they don't receive a pass and wonder why. If they had given the passer a better target — particularly for shorter players — it's much easier for 1. the passer to recognize that they are open and get them the ball, and 2. for them to receive the ball away from the defender's pressure. A defender would conceivably have to go over the back of the offensive player to deflect or intercept the ball. This is a great habit to get into, that will save you a bunch of turnovers and get you more possessions with the ball in your hands.

A Sneaky Way for a Short Guard To Get a Steal off of a Made Free Throw

A sneaky way for a short guard to get a steal off a made free throw is to hide behind the person taking the free throw. After the basket is made, you can sneak out into the passing lane and grab an easy steal. This is particularly effective if you do it when there is a post player or a bigger player shooting, and in an end-of-the-game situation when you need a steal and the other team is frenzied, rushing to get the ball out of bounds before pressure might be set up, and they are not fully paying attention. If you hide behind that player and you knife into the passing lane as the ball is coming out, you can often get a nice, easy steal, followed by an easy basket. Then, you can get right into your press and hopefully have them frazzled enough to get them to turn it over again.

The Best Way To Beat a Double Team (Quickly Get Rid of the Ball and Rotate It)

The best way to beat a double team is to immediately step through and split the two defenders and attack the basket. This should draw a third defender to you, so you almost always will have an open person near the hoop that you could pass the ball to for an easy look. It is important for you to understand this when you are in that situation so you know to focus on finding the open man. Short of that, if you cannot immediately step through and break the double team with your dribble, you need to identify where the double team is coming from and immediately pass the ball to the person who's left open. Then, if he doesn't have a good shot right away, especially if he's further from the basket, he needs to rotate the ball to his other teammates, as well. As the defense tries to recover and get back in position, eventually, you're going to find a mismatch, where you will get an open look for an easy basket. The concept to remember is the quicker you and your teammates rotate the ball the more likely you will catch the defense out of position when they are attacking and double teaming the ball.

The Best Kind of Compliment

The best kind of compliment is at the end of the game, when you're going through the handshake line and everybody is just saying the perfunctory, "nice game, nice game, nice game." When the person who was checking you the majority of the game, or whom you were checking, stops and grabs you and instead of "nice game," says "you played a really good game," or something similar — he singled you out from the rest of your teammates and made sure to let you know that you played a great game, you gave him a hard time, or whatever it may be. You should strive to get that kind of respect after every game. When you earn the respect of your opponents, that's the best compliment you could have.

I remember playing as a wide receiver in a high school football game in which I only caught two passes because we were mostly a running team, but we ran the ball to my side a lot. My job was mostly to block the cornerback, and I played hard every down. I remember that after the game, the guy playing opposite me took me out of the handshake line and said, "man, you were the toughest wide receiver I went against all year." I never forgot that and from that point on, in every game I played, no matter the sport, I strived to earn the respect of all my opponents.

Mom Is Always Watching—Make Her Proud

The thing to remember about moms is that they are always watching, whether in the stands, in heaven, or in your heart. It is valuable to remember this, because during a game, it is easy to take the opportunity when the ball is not near you to take a cheap shot, or to talk back to a referee, or do something else that your mom wouldn't be proud of. If you always make it a point to play like your mom is watching, even if she's not in the stands, you will most likely never run afoul of having bad decorum in a game. You will avoid getting in trouble with your coaches or your teammates, or any other repercussions that it may cause. It can help to always think: would you want to make your mother proud, or would you want your mom to be mad at you for doing something that's not appropriate in a game? You should always strive to make your mom proud and not embarrass her.

CHAPTER 8

Tips for Coaches and Parents

How To Responsibly Handle Cuts

When it is necessary to cut young athletes who try out for a particular team, it is important to base these cuts on the player's ability to play basketball, and not on who is friends with whom, etc. The appearance of bias in selecting a team roster can lead to hard feelings and create unnecessary tension in a school or outside community. That is why it is best to avoid any appearance of favoritism, if possible. One way you may be able to accomplish this would be to ask a local active or retired high school coach to watch tryouts and give you his or her opinion on who should make the team.

The way cuts are handled can have a lasting negative effect on a child's confidence and feeling of self-worth. When cuts are made, I suggest that the coach meet privately and individually with each child to inform them whether or not they made the team. This can be a very stressful and anxious time in a child's life, and care should be taken to be as forthright and honest as possible with each child to their face. I do not recommend singling them out by posting a cut list for everyone to see, or sending them home with a sealed envelope letting them know if they made the team or not.

When meeting with those who did not make the team, make as concerted an effort as possible to be constructive in your feedback about why they didn't make the team and what skills they need to work on in order to make the team the following year. It would also be helpful to have registration forms or information available about alternative teams, like local recreation teams where that child can choose to participate and work on improving his or her game.

Additionally, some coaches may want to offer the kids who were cut the opportunity to practice with the team (especially if they are underclassmen), so they can improve their skills for the following year. As an added benefit to the coach, if a child or two who made the team gets injured or for whatever reason can no longer participate, you will have a player(s) available who can step right in. If they are underclassmen, the practice time will in most cases prove to be valuable in getting them better prepared to be on the team the following year. A coach can also offer those who are cut the opportunity to be a team manager or statistician (particularly upperclassmen). This may not only be gratifying to the student, but prove to be helpful to the coach as well.

Good Game Decorum and Sportsmanship Tactics

It is very important that coaches be good role models and display good sportsmanship during games. If your team has a big lead against an obviously inferior team and the other coach begins to sub his bench in, that would be a good time to call off your press or take your star player(s) out. Oftentimes, you may be able to exchange glances or even tell the opposing coach you are going to be subbing your bench in so he has an opportunity to match up his bench players against more evenly matched competition without the risk of hurting those kids' confidence.

Whether your team is winning or losing big, and you begin to sub players in from your bench that do not have a lot of experience, it is a good coaching tactic to initially leave at least one seasoned player in, or even gradually mix in your subs with the starters so they do not get overwhelmed and lose confidence. Typically, the point guard or a good ball handler is an ideal player to help settle down the subs and keep control on the floor.

It is also important for your players' development and their psyche to define each player's role on the team. Every player should have a clear understanding of what is expected of them. This will not only be beneficial to the players, but if done correctly, it can help foster team harmony and unity.

Every kid doesn't have to play every game, but an effort should be made to not single out only one player who does not get into a game. If it is necessary, you can use a time out to get a player(s) into a game before it is over. If the game has been decided either way, there really is no reason why only one child shouldn't get a chance to play if all his teammates have gotten a chance.

The Best Way To Handle Officials

As a coach, first and foremost you should strive to be a good role model to your players — one that sets a good example for your athletes to emulate. There have been far too many incidents in recent years of sideline behavior that not only sets bad examples for your players, but quite frankly is embarrassing to the entire coaching fraternity and athletic community. Yelling at or berating an official, an opposing player or a coach beyond reasonable levels is quite simply not acceptable behavior for a coach.

A good way to remain respectful to an official and set a good example is to politely ask about a particular call that you have a question with, versus yelling and screaming at him or her. The added benefit of this is you are more likely to be the beneficiary of a future close call, than if you "ripped" the ref's head off. Please also make a concerted effect to keep the use of profanity to an absolute minimum as it sets a very bad example to your players, and there really is no place for it on the court. Rivalries are fun and exciting, but please remember to be respectful to your opposing coach and players, win or lose.

Coaches: you give so much of your own time and energy to share your love of sports with your players, I hope you will use this as a guide to make the coaching experience better for not only yourself, but for your players, and your opponent's players as well.

How To Keep Parents Engaged and Supportive

The single most important thing a coach can do to keep parents engaged and supportive is to be very transparent with communication. A great way to do this is to get all of the parents' email addresses and include them on most, if not all, communications with the team. This includes sending out updates after every game, what is on tap for the upcoming week, schedules, etc. Do not have a parent wondering what the schedule is going to be, because parents have lives too, that they need to schedule around, and if you make things difficult for them to figure out, they may have an attitude toward you just because of that. Conversely, if you make things very easy and transparent for them, they're going to appreciate you that much more. For instance, if they have a child that isn't getting the playing time that they'd like, they may give you the benefit of the doubt just because you have been open and upfront about everything with them from the start.

Additionally, you want to share little insights with the whole group that you might share in the locker room, so parents can get a little inside info on who is stepping up. You may make a comment like, "Darnell really picked his game up in practice this week and it really showed in the game, and that's why he got extra minutes." That may end up answering a question of a parent that was wondering why their son didn't play as much as he usually does. Little things like that — just the act of showing transparency — can go a long way. Make it a point to always be positive in these emails. Do not try and bring down a particular kid or any number of kids in these emails. Additionally, for any team building events, whether it's a pack-the-gym type of event or a long road trip that you are going to make a long weekend out of, anything that you're going to do as team building, try to include parents as much as possible. Have an open dialogue with them to make them feel a bit of ownership for the team and the team's success.

I've seen this happen with one of my sons' small prep school. They had such a small student body that they didn't have enough students to field a cheerleading team. The boys' basketball team was so wildly popular and successful that the moms, appreciative of all the communication and inclusion by the coaches, banded together. They made fatheads for the kids, bought themselves shirts and skirts that matched the team colors and basically became the de facto cheerleaders. They attended every game, home and away, to cheer on the team. Not only was it great for the players and coaches, but it caused great engagement among the parents, and ultimately led to a tight-knit basketball family and a very successful season.

If a parent does approach you regarding playing time, do not automatically be defensive. Tell them that you would love to sit down and speak with them in private. Be fair and upfront with the parent. By being frank, you may help resolve a lot of questions. It could be something as simple as, "John is showing up late for practice every day," "isn't giving his all in practice," or, "is constantly screwing around." Whatever the reason, stating it clearly will be helpful to both you and the parent. This is a great opportunity to even enlist the parent's help. You could offer, "if you could help me get Dave to be more responsible or more dedicated, that will help me put him in the game more." Now, instead of a detractor, you've gained an ally, who will hopefully help you get their son on the right track.

There are times, on the other hand, that you may need to be open-minded to what the parent is saying. They may have some insight that can be helpful to you. It could be that their child has been struggling with an injury or something else and they were too afraid to let you, the coach, know. You should thank the parent for letting you know, and encourage them that your proverbial door is always open. Then, if appropriate, you should make it a point to approach the player and let them know it's okay to tell you as well, and modify whatever may be needed to help that player out.

Institute a Defensive Point Club

One thing that I have implemented at both the high school and recreational level to increase effort and competition on the defensive side of the ball is a defensive point club. A defensive point club establishes point values for specific defensive stats that are kept track of during the game. The premise behind this is to get players as excited about "scoring points" on defense as they do on offense. The values increase according to the difficulty in getting a particular stat, for instance taking a charge is worth 4 points, whereas a deflected pass or a rebound are worth 1 point. The other categories that I use are blocks, (1 point), contested shots (1 point), steals (2 points), dive for a loose ball (2 points), dive and get a loose ball (4 points), steal and score (4 points), and the only offensive stat is assists (2 points).

Through trial and observation, I added assists to the club because a tendency I sometimes observed was that a player would get a steal and try to force scoring a basket on it, because they knew they could get 4 defensive points for it, instead of 2 for just the steal. The better play is to hit their teammate with a pass for an easier layup. By adding assists, players can still get 4 points (2 for the steal and 2 for the assist), but by making the better basketball play. At the end of each game, I or one of my assistants will tally up the categories for each player, giving them their total defensive points scored for the game. I also keep a running total for the season and post it in the locker room, and email it to the players and even their parents as a way to share with them how their child is doing in comparison to his teammates.

I have found the defensive point club to be very effective at increasing teamwide defensive intensity. It also almost eliminates players "taking off" possessions on defense. It is a great analytical tool for coaches to see who their most effective defensive players are, and most importantly: it gives confidence to players who do not score a lot offensively, and lets them see how they are contributing to the team's success in their own way. I will usually commend the players who have good defensive games and give an award at the end of the year to the player who has the most defensive points on the season. This creates a competition where the kids are striving for all the defensive points they can get, from the beginning of the first game to the end of the final game.

Often, at the end of a game, instead of worrying about how many points they scored, kids will run up to the stat keeper to see how many defensive points they had. I will sometimes ask injured players or kids on the bench to track the stats for the defensive point club as a way to keep them engaged in the game and to see firsthand the impact of what hustle and good defense can do for their team. See below for a sample defensive point club stat sheet. I just create an Excel spreadsheet and update the totals after every game. You can also use a Google Docs spreadsheet that you can share with players, parents and assistant coaches in view-only mode (see the sample below).

HIGH SCHOOL DEFENSIVE POINT CLUB

Opponent   **Date**

Name	Assists	Rebounds	Blocks	Deflected pass	Steals	Steal and score off it	Taking a charge	Dive for loose ball	Dive and get ball	Total Points
Points	2	1	1	1	2	4	4	2	4	
Jamal										
Rafael										
Anthony										
Jaiden										
Colby										
Rohan										
Neel										
Evan										
Joey										
Casey										
Adam										
Sam										
Chase										
ManMan										

Be Kind

I know that it is the belief of many that part of the role of a coach is to instill discipline and build character in his or her players. Many times, this involves "tough love," often meted out via punishments, tongue lashings, or benching. I do not espouse to the recent politically correct phenomenon of "everyone gets a trophy," and I do believe that kids are better served when they have to work hard to earn playing time, etc. However, I have seen far too often coaches who neglect to give kids a chance to play even if a game is out of reach either way, or worse, berate the kids on the bench (who haven't played) about something done by the kids playing. You may not think that putting a kid in for only two minutes or even 30 seconds at the end of a game will matter to them, but it does. Making the decision to not let them play at all can affect them emotionally — and deeply — and can lead to loss of self-esteem, decreased desire to play, and even depression.

It is very hard for a 10- or 11-year-old (or even a teenager) to mentally accept this type of rejection, especially those yearning for acceptance or wanting to feel like they are part of the team. Remember that these kids, especially on competitive teams, spend hours upon hours practicing and thinking about playing. It is very hurtful to them to feel cast aside or not given a chance. A good rule is to treat all your players like you would want another coach to treat your child, or nephew/niece (you get the idea). Please be kind and do your best to be fair when possible and give every kid on your team a chance to prove himself and play.

Coaches should strive to be a net positive in all the lives of the kids that they coach and not someone who causes a kid grief and pain. If you are a kid who feels like your coach is not giving you a fair shot, photocopy this section and privately give it to him, and politely ask him to read it because you feel like it describes you. Also, remember it is only a game and you will have other chances. No matter what happened in your game, it is never the end of the world. Try to turn your frustration into a positive: to motivate yourself to practice a little more or to practice harder so you can gain your coach's confidence when you do get a chance. Coaches: remember, no game is worth a kid's misery. In recent years, there has been an increase in youth suicides (some as young as age 11). Keep this in mind when interacting with your players.

Players: remember, nothing is ever so bad, even if you feel absolutely terrible, for you to contemplate taking your own life. Things change all the time, and after a day, or even a few hours, whatever was upsetting you at the time will have usually passed. If you ever have these types of bad thoughts, please go talk to your parents, an adult you trust, an older brother or sister, or even a guidance counselor or teacher at school. Many times, just being able to express what is bothering you to another person is all it takes to make you feel better or put yourself into a better frame of mind. Above all, don't hold it all in to yourself. Get what is bothering you out and you will feel better. Trust me on this one, no matter how bad you think things are, as time passes, things *always* get better.

Outside of their parents a coach is often the most influential person in his players' lives and how you treat them can impact them greatly. For example, try not to publicly humiliate a player (in front of his teammates or fans) and if you do (we all have), take the kid aside and let him know you got carried away in the moment and not to take it personally. The 20 or 30 seconds it takes you to do that can mean the world to your player.

Parents, Be Patient

With the competitive nature of sports these days, we are seeing an increased outburst of both verbal and sometimes physical confrontations between coaches, parents, athletes, administrators, and game officials. Obviously, this is a trend that needs to change, by cutting off potential confrontations at the pass by using sound and practical courses of action for any frustrated or disgruntled player or parent. Every parent has a bias for his or her son or daughter and that is normal, but try not to jump to conclusions after one game or a particular game, either on your child's performance or how he was used by his coach. I know this may be extremely hard at times (I have been there), but it is always best to give both the coach and your child the benefit of the doubt before making waves. If this becomes a recurring theme and you feel like your son may be getting overlooked and is "catching more of the coach's wrath" than anyone else, it may be time to approach the coach. The very first thing I would caution all parents in this situation to do is to ask their son or daughter if they feel the same way that you do. Very often, a parent's perception is much different than their child's. Many kids may have come to terms with their standing on the team, and have accepted it as such. A parent trying to intervene on behalf of his or her child may only alienate you from your child, his coach, or both.

If both the child and adult agree that the coach's treatment is undeserved and more playing time should be given, you can approach this two ways. The first way is a kind of self-disclosure exercise for you both. Ask your child if he is picking up everything his coach is trying to teach him, does he hustle at all times including practices, does he fool around in practice or on the bench, does he work on all the parts of his game (especially the ones he is deficient in), are there players on the team playing more than him who are faster, better shooters, or better defenders. This may help pinpoint not only why your son may be experiencing a lack of playing time, but also point him in the right direction to correct any deficiencies, so he can contribute more to his team on the court this season.

If the first exercise proves futile, there could be more going on than meets the eye. This leads us to the second step in tackling this situation. Have your son approach his coach politely and ask him what he can do to improve his game so he can help the team more (i.e., play more). It may be that your son needs to work on consistently getting back on defense more, boxing out better, or simply learning the plays better. This will often solve the problem if the athlete works to correct his deficiencies.

I would recommend having the parent himself only approach the coach as a last resort, as most coaches would love for their players to sincerely ask them what they can do to improve their game. The coach may also notice your son more and offer extra help once he has shown a willingness to improve. If you still decide to approach the coach yourself, from experience, I would advise not trying to corner the coach after a tough loss or difficult game, when emotions are running high. Wait until the next day, and meet privately and calmly, as to not embarrass your child or annoy the coach by publicly berating him. Another important tip: if you're going to talk to anyone, always go to the coach first. Try not to immediately march off to the principal's or athletic director's office, as that will just alienate your child and yourself.

I would start any of these conversations off by thanking the coach for his time and asking him what your son can do to increase his playing time. Be cordial and direct, and offer to help point your child in the right direction. I have found that having the patience to give the team and coach time to evolve will often resolve these problems after a few games. But, even if it doesn't, by being patient you will most likely have a better outcome for your child and yourself than jumping down the coach's throat after the first or second game. It may simply be that your son is new to that coach and he is playing kids he is more familiar with to start. As he gets to see your child perform, he may begin to play him more often.

Not-Your-Father's Drills To Build a Winning Team

In this section I am going to review drills that should be mostly original or have a fresh take on a drill familiar to the vast majority of those reading this book. If you are a player or a coach, we all know most of the traditional drills that are out there, so it is not necessary to repeat them here. This section is designed to give coaches and players a unique look at some novel ways of developing skills that they have not seen before. Additionally, I have listed several online resources and trainers that can provide you with programs and or lessons to improve in the typical way.

Twist to Jim Calhoun's Famous Box Out Drill

Former UConn Men's basketball coach Jim Calhoun is famous for a very demanding rebounding drill that pitted two players against each other on the block trying to box each other out. What made it so demanding is that to get off the court, you had to secure two consecutive rebounds. If you got one and then your opponent got the next one, you would go back to zero and you would stay on the court against the next player in line until you get two rebounds in a row. Legend has it that many players had to endure an entire circuit of their teammates before getting the requisite two rebounds. You could be as physical as you wanted to be, short of punching your teammate, and there were no out of bounds, meaning every inch of the court was in play. It comes as no surprise that Calhoun's UConn teams were known for their grittiness and physical play.

I loved the concept of this drill and used it often as a high school coach to improve our rebounding and to instill toughness, hustle and aggressiveness. Still, I saw that some players continued to rely on out-jumping their man for a rebound versus boxing him out in a game, so I came up with a variation to instill the skill of boxing out. In this variation, everything in the drill is done the same way Coach Calhoun designed except the players cannot rebound/grab the ball until it has bounced on the court at least once. This forced my players to learn how to make contact (see Chapter 3, Section 1) with their opponent (hit) and to use their lower body and buttocks to hold them off and move them until the ball bounced. This proved to be very effective in creating better rebounders. To make this drill even more challenging for advanced players, you can require that the ball bounces twice before it can be rebounded. I also will sometimes do this drill by creating teams of two and require the team securing the rebound to successfully execute an outlet pass to another teammate stationed around half-court for it to count. I still make them hold their box-outs until the ball has bounced at least once.

Sharp Angle Finishes

A very important skill to learn is how to finish at the hoop. As I note in Chapter 6, one of the hardest layups to make is the straight-on layup just from the right or left of the hoop. If you do not angle your shoulders to the square before your release, the ball is going to come right off the backboard for a miss. Because most players only practice layups either on their own or during their team practice from the wing, many players are not used to taking layups at this angle, yet it is a shot that they will often take during games. This drill will help you increase your shooting percentage on these shots and increase your overall scoring.

You should start this drill on the center of the foul line and take one aggressive dribble to the right side of the hoop, dribbling and finishing with your right hand, being sure to square your shoulders when you release. You should grab your rebound and dribble back to the foul line, and attack the same way from the left side, dribbling and finishing with your left hand. Do this continuously for 20 total reps, 10 on each side, and keep track of how many you make. Use that as a benchmark to meet or beat the next time you use this drill.

For advanced players, or once you become proficient at this drill, you can start each attack with a crossover — or some other attack dribble move — or have a friend stand under the middle of the basket with his hands up (don't have them try to block the shot). Also, you can try a one-handed scoop finish instead of just a traditional layup, as that shot may be easier to get off for players at a higher level of competition.

Finishing in Traffic

It is difficult to consistently recreate the traffic and difficulty of finishing in the paint during a normal practice with enough repetitions to see steady improvement among your players. So, I devised this drill while I was coaching in high school to increase confidence in finishing offensive rebounds in the paint. It simulates quick-twitch jumping, that coaches love, and improves the agility and confidence of my players. This drill can also be done with one or two partners for players working out on their own to get better, but it is mainly designed for use during a team practice.

First, divide your team into groups of three, by height, then assign each group to their own basket — if your gym only has two baskets, you can assign multiple groups to each basket and rotate groups. The players should set up for the drill by getting in a line at the foul line. The first player tosses the ball off the backboard for the next player to catch and throw off the backboard without landing, like a tip drill, while the third and last player in line catches the ball and then has to score by putting it right back up without dribbling. The two players in front of him turn and put their hands up on defense, but they do not try to block the shot. The player shooting has one chance to score and then once the ball is scored or rebounded, the drill begins again with everyone moving up a place in line.

This also teaches players not to bring the ball down in the paint where a smaller player can steal it or tie him up. I would usually run this drill continuously for several minutes until I felt everyone had some success with it. I would sometimes have the players keep track of the score, with the winners having to run one less sprint at the end of practice. In that case, I would have them do five or seven rotations, ensuring everyone had an equal number of chances to score. That usually made for a much more intense drill.

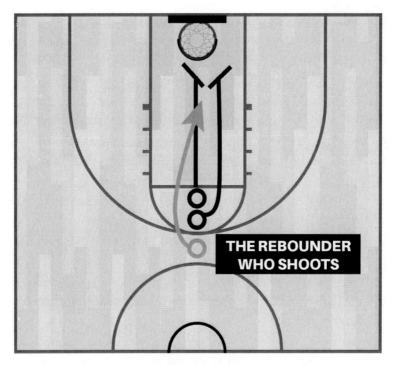

THE REBOUNDER
WHO SHOOTS

Finishing in Traffic

One of my favorite outside-the-box drills is "layups with a chaser," because you can quickly and easily see the results of this drill pay off in a game. I love it for both players just starting to learn how to play and for advanced and older players, because it recreates a common game situation. We have all either witnessed or experienced a seemingly open fastbreak opportunity, when out of nowhere, a player on the other team hustles down to distract the shot just enough for it to be missed — whether it was nerves or just getting surprised that caused the miss.

This drill tries to replicate making layups with a defender bearing down on you in a game, and to build confidence in players' ability to convert the layups in these situations, because it is very rare to get a wide-open layup with the perfect angle in a game. To use this drill, have one line start at half-court near the right sideline, and have a second line of evenly divided players about 10 feet behind them and to their left. A coach who will be the passer will be standing next to the first line, on the right sideline. When the drill starts, the coach will pass the ball ahead for the first player to track down and finish with a layup. At the same time, the first player in the second line sprints down hard behind the player trying to score. He can stomp his feet, yell, or wave his hands to distract the player with the ball, but he is not to try and block the shot. After the play, the player following the shooter rebounds the ball and dribbles it back to the coach and the players switch lines (I will use two or three balls for this drill). I will usually run the drill until everyone on the team makes a layup in a row, without anyone missing, then I will switch the drill to the opposite side of the court. Finally, I'll run the drill from center court, so they can also get used to finishing directly at the hoop, which happens a lot during games.

A variation of this drill is to have the coach pass the ball from center court to the player cutting at the 3-point line, and he should try to take only one dribble to finish. As in the previous drill the players in the second line will sprint down hard behind the player trying to score and stomp their feet, yell, or wave their hands to distract the player with the ball, but they are not to try and block the shot. I usually use this as the first drill of practice, because it loosens up the players and sets the tone for the rest of practice. As the season progresses and the players get more proficient, it will take less time to complete, with everyone making a basket in a row.

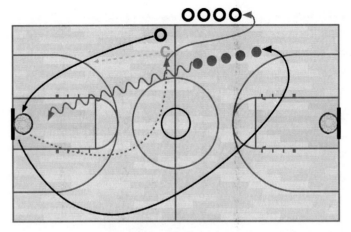

Layups with a Chaser

Single Exchange Passing

Spending valuable practice time on competent passing and catching is often overlooked, but when your team is not very good at it, they will most likely struggle with turnovers and create opportunities for your opponents to score. I like this drill because it can be done quickly and efficiently while bringing a nice quick tempo to practice. It is easy to do — simply divide your team into two lines about fifteen feet apart and facing each other. I will usually set the lines up so players of the same height will be passing to each other. This drill uses only one ball. It starts with a chest pass and the player receiving the pass runs toward the passer, catches the ball, then immediately makes a chest pass to the next player in the opposing line, while still moving. Once a player makes a pass, he sprints to the end of the opposite line. I will usually require that 10 or 20 passes are completed in a row without any drops, bad passes or flubs, before we can go onto the next pass. Once we get the required number of passes in a row, we immediately transition into the next pass which is the bounce pass, then the overhead pass, a one-handed side pass (which I will explain below), a touch pass, and finally, quick hand-offs. Throughout this drill, I emphasize quickness, the receiving player giving a target for the ball, and clean, crisp, fundamentally sound passes.

A one-handed side pass is a newer pass that has come into vogue in recent years and is mostly for wing players to be able to receive the ball and quickly move it to a player in the corner before a defender can react. This gives the receiving player a split second longer to get his shot off. In a game, when the wing receives the ball, he quickly uses his hand closest to the intended player to pass it without turning his body to face the player. When doing the drill above, the player passing will need to turn sideways before making the side pass for it to recreate a game-type scenario.

Redirecting Ball Handlers on the Break

For this drill, station two players at the foul line, one with the ball facing half-court and the other facing the baseline. When the coach yells, "go," both players will move in the direction they are headed as fast as they can. The ball handler should dribble to half-court and then turn around and attack the basket as if he was on a fast-break. The defender should touch the baseline and then try to defend the ball handler trying to score. The coaching points for the defender are: don't over-attack the ball handler letting him go right by you, but instead, come out in a controlled manner where you can make the ball handler slow down or change direction off his intended path. This is done by positioning yourself to force him to change his intended path to the basket. By forcing him toward one of the sidelines, even if it is just momentarily, you gain valuable time for some of your teammates to get down the court to help prevent an easy basket.

If you get him to give up his dribble, then get right up on him with your hands up to prevent a shot or a pass to a cutter.

When you attack the ball handler, angle your feet and arms to one side to keep him from going on a straight path to the basket. If you attack with your feet level to the ball handler, it will be easy for him to crossover and go right by you. Ball handlers who are most effective at getting by defenders in an open-court fastbreak situation do so by making one quick move and getting back on a straight line to the hoop. More information about redirecting ball handlers on the break can be found in Chapter 2, Section 4.

Redirecting Ball Handlers on the Break

One Hand Passing Drill

This drill can be done with a partner or you can use a wall as your partner. The two players stand about 8 to 10 feet apart from each other in a good basketball stance, with their knees bent and their feet shoulder width apart, and each has a ball in his right hand with his left hand up.

When you start the drill, both players will simultaneously pass the ball with their right hand to their partner's left hand. The players should catch the ball with their one open hand and then pass from that hand to their partner's open hand. Once you complete about 10 of these, switch to bounce passes. After 10 of those, make it more challenging by bouncing the ball once before passing it high, and then after 10, bounce it before making a bounce pass. Then you can dribble once, cross, then pass. You can also try between the legs, cross, pass, or: dribble, cross, cross, pass, or: behind-the-back dribble then pass. In the same setup, you can have one of the players make a chest pass while the other makes a bounce pass, then switch after 10.

Then you can try each player making a simultaneous behind-the-back pass, first with their right hands and then with their left hands. You can also use just one ball and make cross passes to your partners opposite hand, so it would be your right hand to his right hand and after 10 reps switch so it goes from your left hand to his left hand. Once you master the mechanics of this drill the key is do it as quickly as possible while keeping control of the ball. This drill will develop confidence in catching and passing and hand eye coordination in your players.

Trainers and Resources That I Recommend

Attending a basketball camp is one of the best ways for athletes to hone their skills, learn new techniques, and gain confidence in their game during the offseason, but not all camps are created equal. Some camps are essentially a bunch of pick-up games and drills with very little in the form of instruction. You can get close to the same experience by going to the park. I like camps that teach fundamentals as well as advanced skills, and teach them so you retain them. Good camps also show you the importance of leadership, being a good teammate, etc.

Look for camps that will "boost your basketball IQ." There are two national basketball camps that I highly recommend for any athletes serious about taking their game to the next level. One of them is PGC Basketball Camps, which carries on the legacy of Dick DeVenzio. One of their stated goals is to teach players to, "Think the game and become the player your coach trusts the most." I have had both of my boys attend PGC camps and have seen demonstrable improvement from each after they attended the camp. I am very familiar with their curriculum and some of their coaches and directors, and both are topnotch. You can learn more about PGC and find a camp near you at www.pgcbasketball.com.

The other camp that I recommend is Breakthrough Basketball Camps because of the way they run their camps through progressive learning. You can see clear improvement in skills throughout each day and from one day to the next. I have worked as an assistant clinician at several Breakthrough camps and my sons have also attended several of these camps. I can say without a doubt that they do an excellent job of fulfilling their stated goal, "helping players quickly develop new skills for scoring, playmaking, shooting, and ball handling with greater confidence so they can make a bigger impact on their teams their next season." All the lead clinicians that I have worked with at Breakthrough camps are thoroughly prepared, super enthusiastic about getting players to successfully learn new skills, and love working with kids. You can find out more and book a camp at www.breakthroughbasketball.com.

There are many local trainers who do a great job in their communities to help develop young basketball players. When looking for such a trainer, ask if you can get a reference or two, and watch a workout before making a decision. At the end of this section, I will list several that I have worked with in different parts of the country that do an excellent job of teaching the game of basketball and its finer points. I will also share with you several national trainers who sell workout videos that I have found to be very helpful. One of them is Collin Castellaw, the owner and founder of Shot Mechanics. You can visit www.shotmechanics.com or his YouTube channel for plenty of free content that I have found to be invaluable for developing offensive skills. I highly recommend his premium products as well, as I have found them to be very effective. Another online trainer that I have seen tangible results from is Coach Rock from ILoveBasketballTV and www.Revengebasketball.com. He also has a wealth of free content on his YouTube channel and website.

Below is a list of coaches and trainers that I have had the pleasure of working with and learning from. I am confident in recommending them because each one has the players' best interests at heart, they all have great knowledge of the game, and all of them do an excellent job in developing and improving basketball players in various places around the country.

Coach Jake Straughan is a skill development and shooting coach for the global brand Shot Mechanics Basketball. He also helps athletes earn collegiate athletic scholarships to further their academic and athletic careers with his company Preps Recruiting. He can be reached at shotmechanicsjake@gmail.com or jake@prepsrecruiting.com.

Coach Adaeze (www.coachup.com/coaches/adaezem) works with male and female players from grades 5 through 12 in the

Greater Bloomfield Connecticut area. She can be contacted at coachadaeze@gmail.com.

Coach Justin Bowen, owner of The G.O.A.T. Sports Academy in Chicago, IL. He can be reached at thegoatprogram@gmail.com.

Coach Ryan Thomas (www.hoopgrind.com) is in Jacksonville Beach, FL. He can be reached at info@hoopgrind.com. If you're not in Florida, be sure to check out the virtual training app on his website.

Coach Dan Horwitz works with basketball teams from youth to college levels, to help them build and sustain a championship basketball culture. He also trains kids aged 8 to 16 who live in the Hartford, CT area. He can be reached at contactdanhorwitz@gmail.com.

Post-Game

At the completion of any game, it makes sense for both coaches and players — individually and as a team — to reflect on what went well and what you or the team can improve upon. This type of post-game reflection, if done honestly and consistently, will almost always result in improved results on the court. In that same vein, after completing this book, I would recommend you do a sort of post-game retrospection of what you read, and take note of what you would like to incorporate into your game.

Now that you are aware of the new tactics, techniques and strategies discussed in the book, make it a point to work on what you learned. Put them into practice so you can see the results on the court. The last few pages of this book were left blank intentionally as a notes section for you to write down the areas you feel could be helpful to work on, or you can use it to make note of sections you feel you may want to go back and review from time to time. Simply stated, if you follow the advice in this book, your basketball IQ will soar. If you consistently work on practicing what you have learned and carry those skills with you every time you take the court, you will win more games. Thank you for trusting me and congratulations on finishing this book.

Acknowledgments

I would like to thank all the hundreds (maybe thousands) of players I have coached over the years. Nothing makes me feel greater than to have a former player greet me as coach when I run into him or her and ask how I am doing. I truly cherish the time I spent with each of you and thank you for allowing me to impart what I know about sports, life and family with you.

To all of my teammates over the years: we played hard, we won (a lot), and most of all we had fun, many of us having forged lifelong friendships. Whenever we get together, invariably the topic of sports comes up and stories are shared of our playing days, bringing back great memories.

Coaching is never a one-man job, and I would also like to thank the many fellow coaches who toiled the sidelines with me over the years. Coaching camaraderie is another one of the joys that a fulfilling coaching career will have, and mine was no different. I'd especially like to mention several coaches who I have coached with who have become lifelong friends: among them Jay, Jason, Joel, Darryl, Nate, Carmine, John, Luigi, Dean, Ollie, Brian, Jeff, Tim, Kyle, and Chris are just some of the guys I have had the pleasure of coaching, strategizing and hanging out with after games over the years.

A very special thanks to two authors without whose unselfish help I could not have done this. Mary Donnarumma Sharnick, author of Thirst, Plagued, Painting Mercy, and The Contessa's Easel: you got me started on my path with your invaluable insight and tips. Dan Horwitz, author of Help Them Up: your motivation, guidance and inspiration got me across the finish line. I will be forever appreciative to both of you.

My Mentors

I consider myself to be extremely fortunate to have been around, coached by and coached against some literal coaching legends in my hometown. I truly never would have been able to become a successful coach or have even half the knowledge I'd need to embark on writing a book like this without them. Between them there is surely 3,500 plus career wins, I truly am lucky to have crossed paths with these men.

They are: Joe Gilmore, my grammar school basketball and baseball coach, Tim McDonald, former Holy Cross High School basketball coach, Hank Spellman Kaynor Tech basketball coach, Ed Generali former Holy Cross High School basketball coach (and my high school guidance counselor), Bobby Brown former Crosby High School basketball coach (and my Mickey Mantle baseball coach), Marty Sparano, former Kaynor Tech basketball coach and Athletic Director, Joe Begnal, former Kennedy High School and Crosby High School football coach and Athletic Director, William Barbarito, former baseball coach and Athletic Director at Kaynor Tech High School, and James Quinn, former boys and girls coach at Thomaston High School. Former coaching opponents whom I have had the pleasure of matching wits against and discussing the game of basketball with: Jack Taglia, former basketball coach at Kennedy High School, Tony Turina, former basketball coach at Torrington High School (and high school official), Dean Acctura, former basketball coach at Woodland High School, Jon Carroll and Billy Martin, former basketball coaches at Sacred Heart High School, and Peter Tehan, former Wilby High School basketball coach. All of whom, by the way, were always gentlemen on the court. There are many more, and I appreciate our time together as well.

About the Author

Jason Calabrese is a former high school coach who has coached at the freshmen, junior varsity, varsity, and AAU levels of basketball, football and baseball. He competed at the collegiate level in both football at Southern Connecticut State University and basketball at UConn Stamford Branch.

He currently coaches in summer and fall basketball leagues and will occasionally scout high school basketball for his coaching buddies when asked to. For the past four years, he has worked as an assistant clinician for Breakthrough Basketball Camps where there is a heavy focus on basketball IQ, as well as on making a positive impact on players' lives either directly or by educating coaches and parents around the world.

All the wins and championships aside, his best accomplishments are having helped build character, grit, determination and sportsmanship in the boys and girls he coached, that they are now able to relate to as young men and women.

For additional resources or to connect with Jason, visit BoostYourBasketballIQ.com.

Notes

Made in United States
Cleveland, OH
21 December 2024

12507050R00065